Diary of A Life

A Poetic Journey

Kimella Hilliard

For Barb,
My friend and
fellow traveller.
With love,
Kim

 FriesenPress

Suite 300 - 990 Fort St
Victoria, BC, V8V 3K2
Canada

www.friesenpress.com

Copyright © 2021 by Kimella Hilliard
First Edition — 2021

ISBN
978-1-03-911507-1 (Hardcover)
978-1-03-911506-4 (Paperback)
978-1-03-911508-8 (eBook)

Poetry, Subjects & Themes, Women Authors

Distributed to the trade by The Ingram Book Company

Table of Contents

For my children, grandchildren,
greatgrandchildren, and future generations,
with love and understanding.
I am in you, and you are in me.

INTRODUCTION

This is the journey of a being who manifested as a female middleclass Caucasian at a time in history and culture that labelled and identified everyone and everything into little boxes of right or wrong, good or bad, and this or that. The best way to read this story is to understand that it has been written by the magnificent three: the mind, body, and soul of one being identified as Kimella Louise Gosse Hilliard. Mind and ego constantly try to separate us from everyone and everything, analyzing and processing to make sense of experience not fully understood. Body—patient and forgiving—allows us to experience the physical manifestations of this journey, through sight, sound, touch, taste, emotion, and movement. Ignored and taken for granted, body gets a lot of abuse and blame for not being what ego thinks it should be, causing a lot of pain and suffering. Soul and Self—the Divine energy of love that is the oneness of all and the truth that quietly resides in each and every one of us—gently and sometimes harshly nudges us and pushes us, waiting patiently for us to wake up and remember. May you find clarity, humour, love, forgiveness, and healing in this journey.

CHAPTER ONE
Setting the Stage

$\mathcal{D}$ear Self,

It is time to harvest the lessons and wisdom this journey has given us, but first, I need to fill in the space when I was too young to write and sound asleep at the wheel.

I arrived on this beautiful planet in the wee small hours of May 31, 1950, in a place called Prince George, British Columbia, Canada. I was welcomed by a young couple who already had a son and would later have another daughter and another son. They were in love, and finding their way in their own lives, which took them many wonderful places but not without their own hardships and lessons.

My first memories are of Prince George and my first home, at about the age of two (give or take a little). I remember being knee high to my mother and watching my older brother being chased by a pig in the pen on the farm we lived on. I remember moving to another house in Prince George and one day feeding my mother's friend's baby dirt as she was sleeping in the buggy outside. I just wanted to do what I had seen them do and feed the baby. I remember going on an adventure with a little neighbour boy with my doll buggy, down an alley past garage doors, and sitting on a grassy ledge on a cliff above the industrial park, totally oblivious to the concerns of my mother. I think we were always seekers—my mind, body, and soul—travelling together blindly, with an undefinable knowing but a quest all the same.

I remember my first memory of physical attributes, when my mother's friend commented on my big brother's beautiful eyelashes, and I wanted them too. I remember my first experience of death at the age of four, chasing baby chicks in the basement of a neighbour's house with other children and someone accidently stepping on one, squishing and killing it.

I remember, at the age of seven, being so excited as I learned to write cursive and so proud of my accomplishment. Then the family moved from Ocean Falls, BC, Canada to Bellingham, Washington, USA, and the school curriculum was different. They didn't teach cursive writing yet, and I had to sit and wait a whole year before I could use my special skill. I was bored and lost interest, and I think that had a lot to do with my lack of drive in the academic department. Comments on my report cards often noted that "Kim is a daydreamer and needs to pay more attention."

I remember starting to gain weight during this time, and as I became heavier, it drew attention and comments from friends and family. Grandpa called me "Tubella" for many years, and I was put on diets and given only restricted treats, so I ate in secret. The message was clear: I was "less than" the approved norm. This message was embodied in a huge way, and it influenced a lot of my choices and caused much pain and suffering.

I remember, at the age of eleven, being on a camping trip with my family and relatives. We were at a lake, and Grandfather had made a boogie board out of plywood to tow behind his little boat. It was my turn. I had a life jacket on and was holding onto the board as he towed me around. My mother was in the boat to watch. Grandpa wanted me to stand up on the board, but I was terrified and just held on. Finally, in anger and frustration, he cut the motor, dropping me into the middle of the lake. A dead fish was floating by and scared me even more. I looked to my mother for support and protection, but she just stood there looking at me, caught in her own father-child relationship. Grandpa wouldn't speak to me until I apologized for not doing what he wanted. It was the moment I knew I was on my own.

I remember, at the age of thirteen, my family had moved back to Ocean Falls, and a minister's wife had come from a neighbouring village to give birth to her first child, staying in our home for a few days after the birth. I got to hold that precious new life, and I knew instantly that I wanted to have a baby too and be a mother.

I remember, at the age of fourteen—having chosen to not be a stellar student—usually having teary discussions with my father about the comments on my report cards. One day, I did not cry, and my father said he was proud of me, as it showed I was growing up when I did not cry. It was years before I cried freely again, doing everything in my power to supress the less-than-favorable emotions, sometimes resulting in inappropriate laughter.

I was raised in a Christian environment with regular Sunday School and teachings, but they didn't speak to my heart and only managed to nurture the shame/blame game. Division and separation confused the process, enhanced by ritual and celebration. Although it was a community that nurtured and sustained my parents their whole lives, the thread of truth that lies in all religions remained hidden until much later when I could embrace the truth in all.

Sexuality was not a topic for discussion, and secrecy made everything mysterious and taboo. There was no place to go for guidance and information, so it was trial and error. Experimentation and lack of boundaries would bind me to shame and judgement for many years. When the day finally came when I thought I loved enough to share my body with "the one," who promised to be my life partner, that person cancelled the commitment, saying that the more he knew me, the more I reminded him of my mother, and he hated my mother. I was devastated to the core. When Mother's response to my broken heart was to say that she was only sorry I had not broken off the relationship first, I fell into a well of "unlovable angst" that would take me on a promiscuous two-year journey of searching for love through physical sharing.

So many memories pour forth when I have time to run the tape and savour and examine the moments. Life with the family I *chose* took me to many beautiful and interesting places, where by the time I came of age to leave the nest and venture out on my own, captain of my own ship, I had moved nine times and lived in seven towns, all on the west coast of British Columbia with a four-year turn in Bellingham, Washington, USA.

As with any life journey, rolling along, I picked up many signals and experiences that wounded me, confused me, shamed me, grew me, shattered me, and left me with a suitcase full of stuff I didn't know what to do with. It was at this point that I stepped out into the world without a map, at the age of nineteen, on my quest to the unknown, hoping to make sense of why I was here. And now, my diary begins—my *Diary of a Life*:

CHAPTER TWO
Setting Sail

Graduating from high school in 1969, there was pressure to declare to the world exactly what I wanted to become and do, and how I was going to make it happen. I had no clue! Under the pretence of going to a college to possibly get a Certificate in Childcare, I packed my blue steamer trunk with everything I owned and headed to Vancouver, BC. Hosted for a short time in a bed and breakfast that I found through the minister of my parent's church, I felt safe for the moment … until I found work at the BC Telephone Company and moved in with a girlfriend who was going to university. Freedom at last. Let the party begin! It was at this time of loose ends and unknowns that I started processing life in poetry.

CHERISH

I have something very special.
I hold it very dear.
I often took it for granted.
I realized that this year.
It shares with me the good times.
It understands the bad.
It is always warm and loving,
Even when I have made it sad.
It has made me one of the luckiest girls
In this whole world, you see.
My very special something
Is my wonderful family.

1969

FEEL FREE

Feel free to sound your thoughts off me.
Feel free to give me love.
Feel free to wander on your way.
Feel free to go from day to day
With no obligations to me.
I feel free to think my thoughts,
Feel free to give you love.
I feel free to wander on my way,
Feel free to go from day to day
With no obligations to you.
In this place of experience and learning,
In this place of love and hate,
In this place of perpetual wonder,
It is no use to wish and wait
For freedom, because freedom is as free you feel.

1970

*A*fter a year of working in the big city, all my student friends were heading home for the summer to work and make money. I decided to follow them and returned to Prince Rupert to work in a fish cannery, which paid great money, and to save for the next big adventure. This is when the plan was hatched to travel and go find myself. I talked a new friend into cancelling her education plans and travelling with me.

In September, we headed across Canada by train to Montreal and flew to Shannon, Ireland. Backpacks with our worldly possessions and traveller's cheques in hand, we stuck out our thumbs and started our journey. Dublin, Ireland, then a ferry to England, and the big city of London. Another ferry to France, and from Paris, we caught a train to Barcelona, Spain, and camped on the beach with a couple of Americans waiting for the next boat to Majorca. We stayed in youth hostels and explored the tourist sights, but our main goal was to join another friend from Prince Rupert who had moved with her two small children to the little village of Deya`. I was looking for something, but I didn't know what it was, so I just kept on searching.

WIND

Hey wind, say wind,
Why do you blow?
When you are not around, wind,
Where do you go?
You are my friend of many feelings.
Your emotions are so strong,
And when you are expressing them,
You take me right along.
When your loving breezes blow,
Gently caressing the air,
You bring to me thoughts of love
And everything so fair.
When your gusts grow stronger,
Your caresses more demanding,
You fill me with the rush of life,
And my thoughts crave understanding.
When you rage with fury,
Your caresses loving no longer,
You fill me with the strength of God.
My love of life grows stronger.
As you express your feelings
Through each day of every year,
I find I do not fear you.
To me you are very dear.

1970

OLD MAN

Old Man! Old man! Where have you been?
Old man! Old man! What have you seen?
Old man! Old man! Where do you go?
Old man! Old Man! What do you know?
Have you lived? Have you loved?
Do you ever cry?
Have you learned? Have you yearned?
Are you ready to die?
Are you rich in wisdom or
Are you poor in wasted years?
Have you reached your peak in happiness
Or mourned the worldly state with tears?
Old man! Old Man!
You are a blessed sight.
You wear your crown, grey with wisdom,
Upon your head just right.

1970

LONDON

Cathedrals rich in history
Where kings are laid in mystery
And the humble people come to pray for mercy.
"Silence. No photography" in this place of sanctity.
Then a holy man says, "Want to buy some post cards?"
Crowded streets with lots of cars,
People crammed into the bars,
The black man calmly taking in abuse.
They'll take your money; you are so far from anything familiar.
They hate you, but they wish they had your shoes.

1970

SPAIN

Proudly walk in this poor land
And soak up sun along the sand;
And all the while, you think
You are really living.
Smiling politely, thinking you can
Become a part, you extend your hand,
But you sometimes wonder
Who is doing the giving.
Time becomes a memory;
If it is good or bad, you still can't see,
And you are not exactly sure
Where you are heading.
Your life you lead from day to day.
You try your best so you can stay.
A return to what you left back home,
You are really dreading.

1970

DEYA`

The sun beams down to kiss me on my head.
The breeze holds me gently in its arms.
The fragrance of fruit and flowers excite me
As Deya` seduces me with all her charms.

1970

AN EVENING IN DEYA`

Here I sit, fag in hand,
Contemplating my swollen gland,
Wishing for long party dresses,
High-heeled sneakers, and golden tresses.
Doodling with coloured felt pens,
Listening to the cackling of neighbouring hens,
Dreaming of faraway places,
Laughing over past disgraces.
Landing ground for bleeding flies,
Sounding board for children's cries,
Scratching my head and drinking tea,
Running to the john to take a take a pee.

1970

GRATITUDE OF A CAT
Dedicated to the feral cats of Deya`

You take the little beastie,
And you let him into your heart,
And he shows his thanks by polluting
The air with a little kitty fart.
You hold him in your arms,
And you stroke his furry head,
And he returns your love by promptly
Going and shitting on your bed.
You try again by feeding him.
You show him the refrigerator door,
And he licks his lips, rubs against your leg,
And barfs all over your floor.
Alas you see it is all in vain,
And you put him out for the night,
And you spend the next few hours
Scratching your wretched-cat flea bites.

1970

*M*y travelling companion and I parted ways shortly after arriving in Deya`. She wanted to see what the world had to offer, and I wanted to find what was in my heart. I stayed on for a few weeks, and then one evening, standing on the terrace overlooking the rustic beauty of nature and history, the message came in loud and clear: "I want a home and family." I activated my open plane ticket and made my way back to Shannon, Ireland, for the flight to Montreal, backpack and newly acquired guitar in hand. Sleeping in the Montreal airport for three days until the cheap train ticket was available, I rode the rails (in the day car) back to Prince Rupert, BC, arriving with one cigarette and a dime in my pocket.

CHAPTER THREE
Ask and You Shall Receive

$\mathcal{D}$iscovering my heart's desire was to have a home and family, I arrived back in Prince Rupert in December 1970 and was welcomed home by family. Christmas celebrated, it was time to find work and get on with the next leg of my journey.

In January 1971, I found work at the Bank of Montreal as a clerk typist and settled into a life of routine and acceptability. There was a man working in the bank doing an accounting-trainee program. We socialized in a group setting at bars after work with all the other Prince Rupert banking staff. One night in March, this man asked me out on a date to a movie. I accepted. Before we were to go out, we had to check on baby kittens at a friend's house. We started talking, and suddenly, he asked me to marry him. I looked at him, and said, "No." How would we live? He explained that he had some money put aside and wanted to buy a home. I asked him if he wanted children, and he said yes but that he wanted to buy the home first. I said, "Yes," and suddenly, I was talking to my future mother-in-law, announcing an engagement to family and friends, and planning a wedding. We never did get to the movie.

In late June of 1971, we were married in a small afternoon ceremony at the United Church. During my twenty-five-year marriage, I was visited by a guide on three separate occasions. The first was a physical manifestation at our engagement party, which was being held in the staff room above the bank. A total stranger walked up to me. He had a 1950s vibe, wearing blue jeans and a white t-shirt with one sleeve rolled up, with a pack of cigarettes folded into it.

He says, "It does not matter if you are in love; what matters is that you like each other," and walks away and disappears. It was only many years later that I realized the incredulity of this encounter.

In September, my husband accepted a transfer with the bank and we moved to North Vancouver. A year later, we transferred again to Victoria on Vancouver Island, where my husband was from and his family still lived. We set about with our plans and bought our first home. In 1973, we welcomed our first daughter. Life with my parents prepared me for a life of moves. We bought and sold houses, building two from scratch, for a total of nine moves. I got good at packing and setting up homes.

In 1974, I had another prophetic experience with a tea-leaf reading. A girlfriend and I went into Victoria to a little café called the Red Swing. There was an older woman there who did tea-leaf readings for donations. My friend and I sipped tea and waited for our turns. When my turn came, she asked me to make a wish. I closed my eyes and wished for a long and happy marriage. She began to speak: "I see the man in your life struggling with a decision. You will have three children, two of one and one of the other. Two of them will be born very close together. You will be married twenty-five years (pause) forty to fifty. You will meet an old friend who you have not seen for a long time."

Now at this time, three years into my marriage, twenty-five years seemed like a long time. My husband was struggling with the decision to sell our home yet again and buy something else. But as for children, we were planning our pregnancies very carefully. When our daughter was two, we decided it was time and instantly got pregnant with twins. In 1976, we welcomed our son and our second daughter, born eight minutes apart.

THE NORTH

I hunger for your sky of passion
With refreshing tears and breath of life
That sometimes smiles and warms my being.
Someday, we will be together.
I fill with excitement when I think
Of all the fishing boats you carry
On your icy sea of grey.
Someday, we will be together.
Your endless coast and rugged mountains
Undisturbed by progressing cities
Take me dreaming of the time when,
Someday, we will be together.

1974

The second guide encounter was ten years into the marriage. Cracks were showing in the relationship, and one evening, we were going out to a theatre performance. On our way out, my husband turned to look at someone, and a voice spoke loudly to me, saying, "Ask him if he is having an affair. If you don't ask him now, you will not get another chance." I asked the question, and his answer was no, but in truth, his heart was engaged outside the marriage.

ONE DAY AT A TIME

One day at a time, that is all I should deal with.
One day at a time, why do I try for more?
I shouldn't expect to know all the answers.
One day at a time, why do I try for more?
I am carrying the problems of five individuals.
It is so overwhelming. Why can't I see?
I can't solve the problems of five individuals.
I am only one person. What is this doing to me?
The last ten years, I have been on a treadmill.
The demands on me have torn me apart.
I have lost sight of the person that existed before.
I have lost sight of the goals I had at the start.
One little hurt and then a few more,
Not being dealt with, wearing me down.
Festering, growing, all out of proportion,
My affections buried, I thought I would drown.
One day at a time, that is all I should deal with.
One day at a time. Oh, why can't I see?
One day at a time, deal with the positive.
Don't dwell on frustrations; set my heart free.

1981

NEEDS

I am a very passionate soul.
I view life from my heart,
But everything is kept inside.
I don't know where to start
To free myself, unlock the door,
To live as I believe.
I am trapped by life inside myself,
And all I do is grieve
For what I need and what I want.
Why can't anyone see?
The body you see standing here,
It really isn't me.
I need to be respected.
I have a need to share
My innermost thoughts and feelings.
I need someone to care.
I need love and attention.
I am beautiful, I want to hear.
Hold me tight, caress me,
And whisper in my ear that
I mean more to you than life itself—
That our love will last forever.
Alas, it is back to earth I fall.
My dreams are put on hold.
The reality is … I feel alone.
My lover's arms are cold.

1993

MISPLACED LOVE

Motorcycles
Wrigley's gum
The smell of the outdoors
The feel and smell of a blue
Leather basketball jacket
Groping, feeling, long passionate kisses
On a sunny afternoon.
First love.
The smell of water
Big blue eyes
Rolled-up shirt sleeves
Wonderful hands
A white convertible
Stolen "trips" to a world beyond
"Babe" I gave to you.
Second love.
Stability
A shirt and tie
A future, children too
A home, high hopes
Brown hair, yellow eyes
With you I said, "I do"
Third love.

1993

*L*ife went on. We worked. We played. We raised our family. Life was good, but in our hearts, my husband and I were worlds apart. In January of 1996, my girlfriend and I were out walking and talking about the distance in my marriage. I was tired and didn't want to know what was going on. I returned home and sat on the couch, and then it happened: the third message from my guide arrived. A loud voice spoke to me and said, "Ask him."

I said, "I am not going to ask him."

My guide raised his voice again and said, "ASK HIM!"

My husband came into the room, and I asked him. The floodgates opened and confusion and misery poured out. After hours of discussion, we decided to separate. It was twenty-five years to the day we had met.

CHAPTER FOUR
New Beginnings

With the conflicting emotions of failure and freedom, I left the family home to start a new chapter. In my new home, I started to explore and create from a place of "I." No longer needing to compromise for the sake of partner and family, I set out to find out who I really was and unpack the baggage I had picked up along the way.

JOURNEY TO HEART

Once upon a time, a little girl
Dropped into space in this old world.
Her mind was hazy but inquiring too,
A journey to take, much work to do.
Unsure but trusting, she took first steps.
The family around her would give her help.
Who was she? Why was she? She did not know.
One day at a time, down life's road she would go.
A skip, a jump, and then a fall;
When she couldn't get up, she would try to crawl.
Messages and insights filtered through.
What was false and what was true?
Bit by bit, her courage grew.
Her exact destiny, she never knew,
But something inside her kept insisting
Life was for living, not just existing.
She dreamt of passion in all she did,
But behind scars and hurt, she sometimes hid.
She found joy in others and daily living.
Love returned when she practiced giving.
And then one day in her deepest pain,
She looked back on her journey and what she had gained.
Her losses and hurts all fell away.
Her trials and failures became gifts that day.
She saw standing before her, her life's goal.
All the fragments came together, completing the whole.
A woman with strength and much love to impart,
She found herself in her journey to heart.

1996

I REGRET

Dear children:

I regret I did not love myself more,
And therefore, was not there for you
As much as I would like to have been.
I regret I did not know myself better,
And therefore, did not make better choices
For you to look up to—to respect and admire.
I regret I was not stronger,
And therefore, sometimes took an easier route
Because I was scared and unsure.
I regret all the pain and confusion
I may have caused you out of my own pain and confusion
While I was growing up myself.
But, dear children, know that I have loved you
The best I knew how at the time,
And when I knew better, I did better.
For this journey
And the love, knowledge, strength, and growth I have received,
I have no regrets.

1996

THE ROAD

The road is one direction.
It goes one step at a time.
The journey is the same,
Even when you have mountains to climb.
The map is in your heart.
If you listen, you will never go wrong.
The mountains you have to climb
Can only make you strong.
When things seem insurmountable,
Just take it day by day.
When you travel with love in your heart,
You will always find your way.

1997

SEA TO ME

The sea, the sea, you call to me:
"Draw near, stand close, look out and see.
All that is past, is now, and will be."
The depth of your soul such a mystery.
Life reclaimed and life anew,
Depths of passion in all you do.
Shades of grey and green and blue,
You evoke emotion in every view.
Days of calm like sheets of glass,
Beckoning playful hours to pass.
Gentle swells bringing dreams en masse,
Angry storms heading for shores to harass.
Tides flow in and tides ebb out.
Your voice in a whisper and sometimes a shout.
You call to me when I am in doubt.
You let me know what I am about.
The sea, the sea, you call to me:
"Draw near, stand close, look out and see.
All that is past, is now, and will be."
The depth of your soul such a mystery.

1997

THE DREAM

I had a dream.
I dreamed there was a man who did not cheat.
He spoke from his heart.
Content with himself, he did not compete
Or crave the approval of other men.
True to himself, he was complete.
He knew his place in this old world.
He could stand together or stand alone,
At one with nature and faith in his Self.
In his own skin, he felt at home.
Not afraid to cry or love or share, he was my dream.
I awoke and he was gone.

1997

THE DANCE OF LIFE

Some people prefer to stand against the wall of life,
Holding onto the firmness
Of what they know.
Some people prefer to race through life,
Not looking in any direction but running ahead
To see what is better, down the road.
Some people take the moment and move with it,
Swaying, holding, letting go,
Slow dancing to the dance of life.

1997

CONNECTED

We are all connected in some mysterious way.
Our pain comes from isolation we sometimes put in play,
Whether deliberate self-infliction or understanding gone astray.
We need to feel connected, a touch, a look, a smile.
Feeling fully connected makes living life worthwhile.
Losing sight of our connections make living life a trial.
We connect not only to people but to nature and the earth.
To music, art, and poetry, our ties receive wide berth.
We are connected by just being, in death as well as birth.

1997

WE ONLY HAVE A MOMENT

Although days may seem long ahead,
They really do not exist.
Neither do the yesterdays,
The regrets, and the "what ifs."
We only have this moment to love,
Give a smile, a hug, a kiss.
It is only in this moment
We have opportunities we must not miss.
Feel the ground beneath you,
Look up into the sky.
Breathe the air in deeply,
Hear the sounds of life's war cry.
Find joy in the mundane,
Beauty in the dull,
Hope in your frustration,
Faith in your own will.
There are no tomorrows, next times,
Or second chances, you see.
We only have a moment—this one.
Make it the best that it can be.

1997

THE JIGSAW PUZZLE

Our lives are like a giant jigsaw puzzle,
Every moment, every experience
Is a piece of the puzzle.
Until we sort through all the pieces
And put them into their proper perspective,
We cannot achieve the total picture.
That is our life's goal:
To put all the pieces in their proper perspective,
To complete the puzzle that is us.

1998

PUT TO REST

It hurt so bad he had done me wrong.
Our life together was twenty-five years long.
In some deep place, I knew it was best
But how do I put twenty-five years to rest?
I cried, I talked, I asked myself why.
How could my marriage have been such a lie?
I made choices, and I knew they were wrong,
But my fear of the unknown and being alone was strong.
He treated me wrong, but I chose to stay.
"Why couldn't he love me?" I would often say.
I knew what I wanted, but he couldn't see.
The life that he wanted did not include me.
When it was over, and the marriage fell apart,
I went back over the years, right to the start.
As our story unravelled, year after year,
The truth of our journey became very clear.
So young with our dreams we wanted to share,
We needed each other; about our doubts, we did not care.
We had nothing to lose and everything to gain;
It did not take long until we were both in pain.
And now I see he did not do me wrong.
I grew on that journey. I became strong.
The hurt I felt was not intended for me.
It was in his own pain he made choices, I now see.

1999

PATIENCE

Don't be so impatient, my child of life.
Your journey is unfolding just as it should be.
Moments of joy, enlightenment, confusion, and strife.
You are where life intended, even if you can't see.
It is time to count blessings, rejoice in the small:
A call from a friend, special tea, a comfy bed.
Hopes and dreams for the future, we can have it all.
Just be patient, savour this moment, don't look too far ahead.
Don't worry about tomorrow; be grateful for today.
We only have this moment to enjoy and to spend.
Give it the best that you can, at work or at play.
It is the small differences, not big accomplishments, that count in
the end.
Today's lesson is here; study it well.
What can we learn? How can we grow?
Do we need to make changes? How can we tell?
Ask the question, be patient; eventually you will know.
Don't be so impatient, my child of life,
Your journey is unfolding just as it should be.
Moments of joy, enlightenment, confusion, and strife.
You are where life intended, even if you can't see.

1999

FRIENDSHIP

Life is a mysterious journey
From the beginning to the end.
The road we travel has ups and downs
And many curves and bends.
Through all the joys and sorrows,
And while life's responsibilities we tend,
The greatest support and gift in life
Is that of true good friends.

1999

KIM'S SONG

Long walks outdoors
The smell of sea air
A cool breeze on the face
The sound of a seagull's cry
The smells of an active kitchen
Simmering soups and stews
Baking cookies and bread
A family meal being prepared
The smell of a wood fire
The warmth and comfort of an open flame
The cozy softness of fleece
The soft glow of candlelight
A good book, someone's story
Music of all types, expressions of someone's soul
Movies of personal journeys
A laugh that makes your sides ache and tears come to your eyes
The soft smell of a baby
Their unconditional love
Their gurgles and giggles
The warmth of a good cuddle
The security of a cozy home

Surrounded by favourite colours and things
Memories in journals
Photographs capturing special people and times
The solitude of nature
The beauty of flowers, colourful and fragrant
The lapping of waves against the shore
The warmth of a sunny day
To have time to explore and ponder
To taste wonderful foods
To hear music and conversation and the sounds of life
To see all the colour and beauty and change in the world around
To love and be loved
To care and be cared for
To reach out and touch
To feel connected and a part of

1999

CHAPTER FIVE
Finding Me

The children are grown and out in the world finding their own way. I have a beautiful townhouse that I love to rearrange and decorate. I have work that is satisfying and pays the bills. I have friends that support me and take me out to play. Now what?

AND

And with birth, we slide, sometimes easily,
Sometimes harshly, into the lessons of life.
And we bring with us lessons of past lives,
Some remembered, some forgotten.
And each day takes us on a journey of learning,
Of joy, of sadness, of light, of darkness.
And we are together, and we are alone.
We are universal, and we are one.
And the gentle passing of the generations before
Moves us swiftly to the forefront of our own mortality.
And with death, we slide, sometimes easily,
Sometimes harshly, into the lessons of afterlife.
And we are the end, and we are the beginning.
We are the circle, and we are immortal.

2001

BUTTERFLIES

Our souls descend to the earth;
Our journeys start through babies' eyes.
We blossom beneath the sun and stars,
Always reaching towards the skies.
And as our life goals are finally met,
Sometimes after many tries,
The beauty of our souls emerge
Like magnificent butterflies.

2001

THE AWAKENING

You have awakened, in my soul,
Feelings I thought were dead.
Passions and desires have moved
Into my heart and out of my head.
Fears of letting someone in,
Being vulnerable, no longer persist.
Boundaries of sharing space and time
Vanished and do not exist.
You have awakened, in my heart,
The desire to share again.
Walls are tumbling down.
I look forward to where and when.
My blood is coursing through my veins;
My heart feels like it will burst.
I feel so high, I must have wings.
New love to quench my thirst.

2002

THE HAPPENING

Something has been happening;
It started in my head.
A week ago, it was a thought,
Now it is an obsession instead.
The thought moved to a daydream,
Embellished by desire;
Soon it was a fantasy,
My body passionately on fire.
Every waking moment,
And even while I sleep,
Visions of perfection
Surface from the deep.
I thought it was a passing fling
But days and days go by.
Scenarios keep rambling on.
I am engulfed in a delicious high.
And so, it seems this happening
Is a precious message from above;
It is telling me I am once again
Open to falling in love.

2002

THE PHOTO ALBUM

As I turn the pages,
Breaking into laughter and sometimes tears,
I see my life before me,
Categorized by events of all the years.
I see people and places forgotten
And some relatives no longer here.
Memories are brought forward
Of times and people I hold dear.
Times of joy and sorrow
Are etched upon each face.
Occasions are all documented,
Each person, time, and place.
I've moved through many phases,
Making up chapters of my life,
From childhood to my youth,
To married couple, mother, and ex-wife.
And although the pages of this album
Are all that is left of times before,
I know, as my life moves forward,
Pages will be added, many, many more.

2002

And then one day I was driving down the highway on my way to work and the message came: "I want to sing." Within a couple of days, a co-worker invited me to a musical event at the Sons of Norway Hall on Sunday night. I was introduced to the "Gettin' Higher Choir" and fell in love with their energy and the music they were singing. I joined them at their Two Toonie Tuesdays over the summer, and in the fall, I became a member.

GETTING HIGHER IN THE CHOIR

While in my car, driving down the Pat Bay,
I decided I wanted to sing one day.
Within one week I had an invite
To Norway House on Sunday night.
Many musicians had gathered there,
All kinds of talent from everywhere.
And then one group set the house on fire,
A small representation of the Gettin' Higher Choir.
Gabi Gabi was one song they sang;
Into the rafters their voices rang.
Only one small part of a greater whole
And still their music penetrated my soul.
I could not sit still; I had to join in.
Song after song, I tried to sing.
And then when it was over, a gift in my day,
An invitation to join on "Two Toonie Tuesdays."
Over the next few weeks, I met with the choir,
Voices joined together, lifting me higher.
Each week the community was a different blend
Yet joyous harmony was always reached in the end.
By summer's end, it was my desire
To become a member of the Gettin' Higher Choir.

Monday night soprano was where I fit in,
A new relationship in community was about to begin.
Connecting with old friends and making new,
A network of information and sharing too,
No matter how tired and stressed with my day,
I was always lifted up and anxieties fell away.
Fragmentation disappeared, and I became whole.
Joy resounded to the depths of my soul.
Outside distractions disappeared with a tone.
My spirit returned to my bodily home.
There were no differences; we all became one
When the universal language of music was sung.
Communication connected; the message was clear:
Everyone lived in harmony here.
Voices raised in the purest love
To our earthly home and the heavens above.
In troubled times, no greater desire
Than to sing in joy with the Gettin' Higher Choir.

2003

THE EVENING WALK

My day is done, and dusk is upon me.
Walking shoes, reflective vest, flashlight to see
The perfect end to a busy day,
A brisk walk to let my stress fall away.
Darkness falls and open space closes in.
A journey of sounds and smells begin.
A siren sounds near—someone is in trouble,
Caregivers to the rescue, travelling on the double.
Someone doing laundry, dryer-sheet perfume I smell.
Dinner is being prepared; I smell grilled meat as well.
Someone is jogging; footsteps sound behind me.
"Good evening" to a dark figure whose face I cannot see.
Home fires burning, wood smoke is in the air.
Lights glow in windows; families gathering there.
Dogs walking owners; cars rushing home.
Headlights blind me, and then they are gone.
Down the home stretch and around the next corner,
My evening walk is nearly over.
Home to the light and the warmth within.
My day is done; let my evening begin.

2003

ODE TO A WOMAN

Who is this woman in the mirror?
My mother can't be standing here.
Through a young woman's eyes is how I see,
But a mature older woman looks back at me.
What are these lines and whiskers of hair?
What happened to my complexion so fair?
Crepe neck skin and hair turning grey—
Monthly hair dye tries to keep it away.
What was once firm and smooth now sags.
Bright smiling eyes are surrounded by bags.
My youth can't be gone; I must not despair.
Are those warts and skin tags growing there?
My childbearing years are almost up.
My saggy breasts overflow their cups.
My internal thermostat has run amuck.
My insides are outside; it is time for a tuck.
This can't be happening! It is so hard to take,
And there are those joints that have started to ache.
People call me "ma'am" now, instead of "miss."
Where have I been? How could I miss . . .
The passage of my youth, that young woman so dear?
It is me I see looking back from the mirror.
Those physical transformations are mine to own.
The woman of my youth has turned into a crone.

2003

VOID

The journey begins
The quest is on
The question is the same
Since the very first dawn.
Why am I here?
What is this journey about?
Who am I? What am I?
More questions and doubt.
Every moment of every day
I fill up with stuff
To appease the hole in my soul.
It is never enough.
The stuff blocks the way.
The journey is slow.
I hit the wall.
There is no place to go.
It was in the void I grew.
It was in the void I knew.

2003

CHAPTER SIX
Reflection

YOU MADE A DIFFERENCE
For my Mother

When I was little, I sat at your knee.
The Bobbsey Twins and Heidi you read to me.
You made a difference.
The smell of cookies and homemade bread,
A song, a prayer, a tuck in before bed.
You made a difference.
A semi-formal for me from your old gown,
You sewed dresses and remade coats when I had grown.
You made a difference.
A cup of tea and time to sit with friends awhile,
No matter how ugly the day, you always had a smile.
You made a difference.
And so, dear Mom, I want you to see
How very important all these things are to me.
You made a difference.

2003

DAD

For my Father

Some years ago, I met a man.
He was big and strong, an icon to me.
He came and went, working hard,
And then one day he went to sea.
Weeks away and weeks at home,
Taking on different roles, he was a mystery.
He cooked, he cleaned, he sometimes played.
He was all I knew a man could be.
A man of few words, a presence all the same,
He completed the circle I called family.
His twinkling blue eyes and mischievous smile,
A man I will always love, he is my dad you see.

2003

POETIC EPIPHANY

Poetry is the music that flows from my soul.
Fragment life notes harmonize until they are whole.
Thoughts drift randomly, poetry trying to unfold,
Sifting, shifting, rambling until my story is told.
Poetry is my heartbeat, the reckoning of my truth,
The telling of my journey started in my youth.
Sense and sensibility, the mysteries of life's call,
The rhythm of the dance of life . . . poetry records it all.
An intimate relationship, heart song and the written word,
Exposed for the world to see; it is my voice that is heard.
A connection to the universe, a footprint in the sand,
An art form to be pondered, strength in an outstretched hand.
Poetry is my song to sing, my story to be told.
It is my peace, my reckoning as my life journey unfolds.
It is my light in darkness, my anchor in the sea.
It is my joy, my tears, my passion; it is the manifestation of me.

2005

FAMILY

We are all related.
We are the human race.
We live on the same planet and
Share the same breathing space.
Blood runs through our veins.
Our hearts beat to the same tune.
We rise to the same sun and
Sleep under the same moon.
Skin is only clothing.
It comes in many hues,
Bodies are only houses
For our souls and what is true.
Differences may define us but
They do not separate us from the tribe.
Unique but still the same,
We are universal on the inside.
Birthright is only experience,
Gifts and challenges along the way
Of our universal journey and
The choices we choose to play.
We are all related.
We are the human race.
We belong to the same family and
We share this time and space.

2005

HUNGER

We are a world that is starving,
But it is not food we need.
It is the human touch, kind words,
Positive actions, a harvest from these seeds.
Touch has been forbidden,
Deemed sexual in every way.
The human race not hugged, nor kissed,
Dies bit by bit each day.
Without the nourishment of human touch,
The spirit goes into decline.
A starving soul cannot flourish.
Kind words are hard to find.
Without kind words, the spirit shrivels.
Seeds not planted do not grow.
A drought in human kindness
Means positive actions will not be known.
Without positive actions
There is no sun to shine,
No thirst-quenching showers
To nurture all mankind.
We are a world that is starving,
But it is not food we need.
It is the human touch, kind words,
Positive actions . . . let us plant these seeds.

2005

A MOTHER'S TEARS

A mother's tears water the roots of a child,
Nurturing care always there
To support and sustain like gentle rain,
Solid earth grounding birth.
A mother's tears start long before birth.
Conception shifts the universe, and
The body swells with anticipation,
Hormonal rages, and sublimation.
A mother's tears claim joy and sorrow
Of yesteryears and promises of tomorrow,
Of what is and what could be,
The hopes and dreams for the child she sees.
A mother's tears fall just because,
No rhyme or reason,
Embracing all seasons of life and times
For every child, not just her own.
A mother's tears cry for her own child within,
Unspoken praise, parental loss,
The birth of herself,
The end of times, and new times to begin.
A mother's tears, the salt of the earth,
A nurturing gift to ground and uplift,
A loving embrace upon the face
Of every child.

2006

RELATIONSHIP

Relationship feeds the soul,
Challenges the spirit, and makes us grow.
Relationship mirrors what is inside,
Posing questions, being a guide.
Relationship stretches boundaries, makes us learn,
A student first then a teacher in turn.
Relationship embraces what we know.
Without relationship, we cannot grow.

2006

BEST FRIEND

Friendships come and friendships go.
People meet and want to know
About each other, stories to share,
A connection made, sometime, somewhere.
A void filled, a helping hand,
A moment of laughter, validation on demand,
A shared journey, work and play,
Until life changes and roads go different ways.
But one friendship lasts, there is no end,
That special relationship of one best friend.
Not circumstantial with a destined goal
But a connection of heart, mind, and soul.
A connection made, together you grow,
Sharing heart songs and all you know.
A relationship of respect, trust, and truth,
An open book to seniority from youth.
Solid support, no judgement call,
Shared laughter and tears, emotions all.
A person you can count on to see you through.
A person you trust to know the real you.

2006

STREET OF SEASONS

I walk a street of seasons.
Spring births the budding blossoms
In soft whites and gentle pinks,
New life and the promise of a future.
Summer warms the days,
Nurturing growth and maturity.
The blossoms give way to the
Rich lush foliage of life's journey.
Autumn arrives in glorious knowing,
Passionate flame and golden splendour
Of lessons learned, reaping
The harvest of life well lived.
Winter falls, and too soon,
I will stand with life-worn branches,
Bare of adornment,
Strong in the reflection of what I know.
It is my autumn.

2006

LIFE BY TENS

Zero to ten: trust and observation
Ten to twenty: foolishness and dreams
Twenty to thirty: trial and error
Thirty to forty: adulthood and expectation
Forty to fifty: work and reconciliation
Fifty to sixty: revelation and empowerment
Sixty to seventy: acceptance and enlightenment
Seventy to eighty: peace and tranquility
Eighty to ninety: wisdom and reflection
Ninety to one hundred: notoriety and grace

2007

CHAPTER SEVEN

Exploration

AND THE WORLD KNOCKS ON MY DOOR

My spirit descends to this place unknown.
I pray for direction on the long path home.
Darkness surrounds me; I look for light.
Moment by moment, I journey, questioning my plight.
And the world knocks on my door.
Scenarios unfold before me. Emotion penetrates my soul.
The challenge is not to be shattered but to keep my spirit whole.
Lessons to be learned, truths to be told,
Tears to cry, love and joy to hold.
And the world knocks on my door.
Fellow travellers I meet, each in their own time,
Messages to share as relationships entwine.
Each season passes; my truth is known.
The path is ending; it is time to go home.
And the world closes its door.

2007

DO NOT PLANT ME WHERE I WILL NOT BE

When my race on earth has been run,
And my need for a bodily home is done,
Cremate my soul's vessel at my birth,
Reduce it to dust to nourish the earth.
Do not plant me where I will not be,
Sail me on the winds; cast me on the sea.
Mourn me not for I am free
Of earthly time and material debris.
From this worldly journey I will depart,
Forever residing in your heart.

2008

I UNDERSTAND

In my birth, you were my mother,
Holding me close, nurturing me,
Singing to me, bestowing actions of love.
In my youth, you were a stranger,
Disconnected by personal paths
But always present in physical form.
In adulthood, you were the matriarch,
Quietly watching as seasons changed,
Smiling affirmation.
In death, I was your mother,
Holding you close, nurturing you,
Singing to you, bestowing actions of love.
Now you are gone, but your actions remain,
And all is as it should be.
The cycle of life.
I understand.

2009

TOO SOON

The body ages but the spirit lives
In youthful time that age forgives.
The eyes shine bright with all to see;
Visions reflected strangers be.
Music plays the soul to dance;
Memory strays to wasted chance.
Too soon this lifelong race is run;
Too soon on earth my will be done.

2009

PANNING FOR GOLD

The soul departs, the body leaves;
Family and friends remain to grieve.
Tears pour forth, wash away the debris;
Nuggets of gold remain to see.
Actions of love and kindness and such,
Heart songs of all the lives that were touched.
Smiles, laughter, and quirks of routine;
Nuggets of gold remain and are seen.

2009

THE BOSS

I am not your boss.
You are not my boss.
I may be your mentor or guide,
If you choose to receive my gifts.
You may be my mentor or guide,
If I choose to receive your gifts.
A mentor or guide is not always
Someone or something you aspire to be.
Sometimes a mentor or guide is a window
To someone or something you do not want to be.
Do not give up your power
To anyone or anything.
Do not hold your power
Over anyone or anything.
I am my boss,
Divinely connected, mind, body, and soul.
You are your boss,
Divinely connected, mind, body, and soul.

2009

THE MASSAGE THERAPIST

A tall, gentle man enters my place,
Bringing his gift of massage to my space.
No verbal communication, just music is chosen;
A sacred space in time is woven.
Nimble fingers search for knots
In muscle and tissue life has made taut.
Lower back and up the spine,
Shoulders and neck, oh how divine.
Tension discovered, massage and release,
My body relaxes, and I am at peace.
Every muscle and joint lovingly travelled,
Step by step, each knot is unravelled.
From back to front, the journey continues,
Arms and hands, legs and feet are probed, every sinew.
My head held gently for cranial manipulation,
All tension releases in joyous sensation.
Arms open to the heavens in a final stretch,
And my spirit soars.

2009

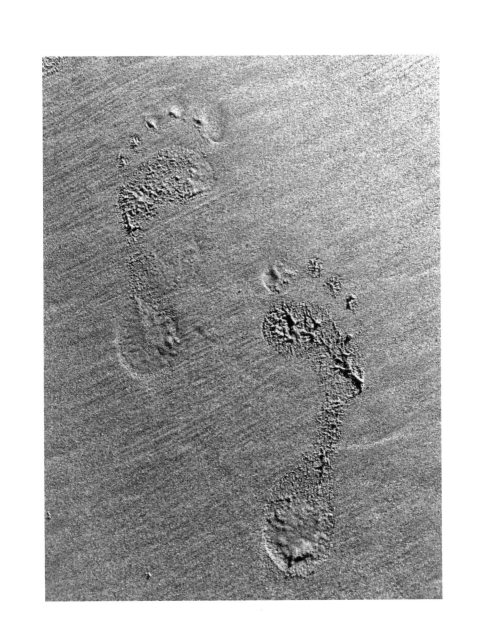

FEET

Unsung heroes, they carry you,
A supportive foundation for all you do.
A reflexology map of your organs path,
A ticklish spot to make you laugh.
They skip, they walk, they run, and they dance;
They play footsies in the game of romance.
A stylish model for fancy shoes
And toenails to polish in every hue.
They are your feet, and time will tell
If you take them for granted and don't treat them well.
A soak, a scrub, a clip, and a buff,
Massage and cream so heels don't get rough.
Proper shoes and socks to protect from wet and heat,
Cherish the unsung heroes, make them happy feet.

2009

EXPECTATION

To have no expectations
Is to never be disappointed
And usually pleasantly surprised.
In learning to accept and experience
The moment we are in
And not tarnish it
With our preconceived notions
and expectations,
we are always ready to receive
the gifts and lessons
intended for us.
We walk the path
We are destined to walk
And become the person
We are destined to be.

2009

THE TRAVELLER

Do not call me by a religious name;
The teachings may differ, but the truth is the same.
I am just a traveller.
Do not identify me by the colour of my skin;
It is only my shelter. I am the soul within.
I am just a traveller.
Do not judge me by how I speak;
My journey is unfolding as my truth I seek.
I am just a traveller.
Welcome the stranger, embrace the friend,
Nourish all with love and compassion until journeys end.
We are all just travellers.

2009

I BELIEVE

I believe I chose to be here
Regardless of the circumstances of my birth.
I believe there is a purpose
In my journey here on earth.
I believe in a higher power;
Call it God, call it Gaia, call it Love.
I believe I have a destiny
Already written by the powers above.
I believe, no matter how dire the circumstances,
There are blessings to be found.
I believe, if I look and see,
There is beauty all around.
I believe that I have choices,
And the outcome is up to me.
I believe. I believe in the human spirit,
And I believe in the power to be.

2009

ENLIGHTENMENT

There is intelligence, a higher power, wisdom . . .
Call it what you may.
It has been called religion, Gaia, consciousness;
It does not matter what people say.
It is the universal truth,
Sometimes the road less travelled.
It connects all beings, all life.
It is the mystery to be unravelled.
Everything is connected;
Nothing stands alone.
I am you and you are me,
And all of life is one.
The path to walk is one of love,
Compassion, forgiveness, and contentment.
As one changes, so do all,
And the world steps towards enlightenment.

2010

FULL CIRCLE

First breath, first sight
Trust, trial, tangible
Declaration, disappointment, delusion
Obedience, oblivion, obvious
Struggle, strangle, salvation
Hurt, heal, harvest
Wrestle, wonder, wisdom
Last breath, eternal sight.

2010

CHAPTER EIGHT
Awakening

A friend invited me to do a meditation retreat at Po Lam, a Buddhist Nunnery in Chilliwack where she lived. I was curious, and the challenge of spending ten days in lockdown and noble silence was something I could not resist. Bets were placed, at the office where I worked, that I would get kicked out for not being able to keep silent for ten days. I made it through the ten days, and very proud of myself, I returned home. Something had changed, something had opened up, and I realized the path of meditation was a path I wanted to continue walking. It became my refuge, my guide, my anchor in the storm, my lifeline to self, and I will always be grateful.

I don't have a lot of time;
it goes in the blink of an eye.
All those dreams still just a thought;
it is now to do or die.

THE ARTIST

I am the artist
I am the work of art
Every step I take
Every choice I make
Is a brush stroke
On the canvas

2010

*O*ne day, in August of 2012, a phone message was left for me at my home that someone was looking for me. They left a name and phone number. I knew the name and returned the call. It was an old friend I had not seen for a very long time. The final prophecy in my tea-leaf reading so long ago. I met my friend, and although we were in our sixties, we only saw the teenagers we remembered. Conversation flowed. There was so much to say and catch up on. A new relationship was born.

MUSIC

I sit in silence, listening for the music of my soul.
With no distraction, I feel the beat ever so slightly.
Mindful, I focus and allow the rhythm to present itself.
Sweet waves of love and joy lift me up
And carry me to great heights.
Life crescendos move me
To anxious expectations, pain, and tears.
I release my expectations and allow myself
To be carried across the stanzas of my life.
This sonata was written long ago.
In silence, I hear it: the music of my soul.
This is my song, and the music is beautiful.

2013

THE GIFT

When the sun seems to be setting on a life of dreams,
And you feel you can dream no more,
Someone arrives at the door of your life,
Bringing sunshine and new dreams.
When day's end looms empty, and you sit alone
In contemplation and reflection,
Someone arrives to sit beside you,
Sharing your memories and creating new ones.
When your cold bed calls you to rest,
Alone with fatigue and the events of the day,
Someone crawls in beside you, holds you close,
Warms your heart, and helps you laugh away your demons.
When you thought you would stand alone
And walk your path in solitude,
Someone steps up beside you, keeping you company,
Side by side, step by step, from now till destined be.
This is a gift.

2013

WALKING MEDITATION

Walking slowly, mindfully
Focus on breath, sensation . . .
A path travelled before,
Familiar but new,
A figure eight walked in repetition,
Stones faded in colour,
Vibrant with the kiss of rain,
Air sweet and fresh,
Cool and bracing.
Landmarks appear,
Calling for recognition:
A three-toed foot, a monkey head,
An old man's face perched on a stone mantle,
Dehydrated lichen alive with neon green
Giving life to dead branches
And crowning the head of a charred stump
In the forest behind the boundary line,
Bare-armed trees, decorated with crystal drops of rain—
"sen-trees" guarding the path,
Reverently embracing the traveller—
One with the earth and sky,
Vibrating energy,
A pulse with no definition or boundary.

2014
Vipassana Centre, Merritt, BC

I AM NOT MY BODY

I am not my body;
my body is not me.
It is my dwelling place
as I travel this earthly journey.
It is my vehicle
to experience the senses:
sight, sound, smell, taste, touch.
It is my teacher
to learn emotion,
love, laughter,
pain, sorrow.
It is my ladder
to climb from darkness
to the light of consciousness.
My body will age;
my soul is ageless.
I am not my body;
my body is not me.

2015

TRANSPORTATION

Our body is our vehicle
To travel through this life.
We cannot trade it in
Or buy a new one,
If we let if fall into disrepair.
We must put the best fuel in it
To maintain optimum performance.
We must move it regularly
To keep it running smoothly.
We must shelter it and keep it clean.
We must detail it and keep it beautiful.
We only get one vehicle for this journey.
It will age and stop.
Take care of it
And enjoy the ride.

2015

WEALTH

They say you can't take it with you:
the wealth of this lifetime,
money, things, stuff.
But when your wealth
is peace, love, joy, happiness,
you do take it with you.
Why would you work so hard
for something you have to leave behind?

2015

EGO

Ego is the shackle of spirit,
The inhibitor of bliss,
The destroyer of freedom.
Ego is a false god,
A fraudulent truth,
A dead-end road.
Release ego and set your spirit free.
Walk into the light
Of your true nature.

2015

TRANSITION

I am still getting used to you,
Getting to know you,
Understanding your patterns,
Passions, and views.
I am trying not to judge,
Form opinions, or criticize.
I wish to walk beside you,
Together and alone,
Sharing, supporting,
Loving, laughing,
Learning, growing.
Sometimes I miss my goal.
Please forgive me.

2015

PROJECTION

I saw a picture
Based on someone's words,
And my own thoughts
painted it carefully
With my pleasures and desires.
I stepped into this picture
And found the words fanciful
And my thoughts creatively directed.
Soft edges became sharper.
The lines became clearer.
The picture changed, and I saw the landscape
With what I needed and knew.

2015

ON BEING HUMAN

What is this saying? "We are only human."
We are human!
And the potential is endless!
We can think and feel.
We can learn and change.
We can grow and be the light of our true nature.
We can choose.

2015

ON OPINION

What is opinion?
Everyone has one,
Forming observation
And experience
Into thoughts or words.
It can never be accurate.
There is always another side,
And things are always changing.
When expressed openly,
Forcing random evolution
Into a solid box of words,
Sometimes hurtful,
Shattering the natural flow
Of observation and experience,
It blocks and diverts the river of life.
That is my opinion!

2015

Opinions,
Unless asked for,
Should be kept
To one's self.

MUSINGS

Judgement creates misery.
Acceptance creates harmony.

My life:
A tangled ball of wool
Unravels
Into a single strand,
Woven
Into a thing of beauty.

I have been wandering
Through the forest
And come into the clearing.
There is a knowing
That cannot be put into words
And articulated.
That is the path
To follow.

2016

LIFE

Life is not just about the magic of first moments;
It is about the shifting sands and the rock of truth beneath.
Life is not just about the excitement of anticipation;
It is about the stillness of what is.
Life is not just about the gratitude of familiarity;
It is about the patience of accepting differences.
Life is not just about the expectation of promises given;
It is about the forgiveness of forgetfulness.
Life is not just about the opinions of presence;
It is about the practice of non-judgement.
Life is not just about the realization of the journey;
It is about acts of kindness and compassion.
Life is not just about what is or is not.
It is about love.

2016

WANDERING

I am wandering
through the forest of my life.
Sometimes the path is clearly marked.
Sometimes I veer off the path
and into unknown territory.
Brambles and branches strike against me,
stinging and bruising.
I push forward and break through
into a clearing
with soft moss to rest upon
and a clear gurgling brook to quench my thirst.
I stay for a while,
embracing the light and beauty around me.
Soon curiosity sparks and I must move on
in search of the next clearing.

2016

THE COMPOSER

I write the story that makes up my song.
I hum that tune even though it feels wrong.
There are always lyrics that even I can't see.
Nothing is exactly as I think it to be.
It is time to stop and listen to the beat of the drum.
Let go, let be, sway to the true rhythm.
Let the life notes lift and carry me.
Let the music of truth set me free.

2016

SEASONING FOR THE SOUL

All that we experience,
see, feel, touch, taste, hear
in this lifetime
is seasoning for the soul.
Sometimes it is bitter, sharp, and pungent.
Sometimes it is sweet, velvety, floral.
The spice of life,
mixing, blending, building the perfect stew
of knowing and enlightenment.

2017

MORE MUSINGS

It is the ego
That feels
Jealousy, anger, and resentment.
The pure heart
Feels only
Love, kindness, and compassion.

Life is fluid,
everchanging.
Don't try to capture it
or put it in a box.
Flow with it.

It is better to plunge into darkness
and search for the light
than to wander aimlessly
in the fog.

2017

THOUGHTS

Thoughts
are only energy
rising to the surface
like effervescent bubbles
in a sparkling drink.
They have no substance.
They roll like a river
of groundless waters
arising and passing away
into the ethos of impermanence.

2017

SOLUTIONS

There is no magic cure
or instant solution.
All healing and wisdom
comes
from a long path
of mindful awareness
and truthful experience.

2017

TRUE LOVE

Societal love
often refers to a relationship
between two human beings.
"Falling in Love"
comes from a place of personal need
and fulfillment expectations.
When things change,
as they always must and do,
the "falling out of love" begins
and relationships are cast aside
and abandoned.
This happens in "love" relationships
to places and things as well.
What the world and all of humanity needs
is to return to the true love
of kindness, compassion, and non-judgement.
The sleeping light in all our hearts,
waiting for us to awaken.

2017

AND MORE MUSINGS

Your life is not defined
By the relationships
You have with others.
Your life is defined
By the relationship
You have with your Self.

With compassion
For ourselves,
We can accept and embrace
Our shortcomings
Rather than denying them
With the closed eyes of the ego.

At some time,
We all crash and burn.
This is necessary,
For then we can rise from the ashes
And become new again.

The flame of passion
Burns inside each and every one of us.
It is how we tend this flame
That determines our quality of life
And whether it burns brightly
Or dims and goes out.

2017

MEMORY OF WALLS

Stark studs and plasterboard,
decorated
with basic paint,
invite first nesting
of the human bird.

Each dweller adds
a coat of colour,
a litany of life
as chapters end
and new ones begin.

Memories are sealed
under layers of paint,
echoes of vibration,
the pulse of life
in the memory of walls.

2017

UNRAVELLING THREAD

Sitting solid,
breathing in,
breathing out,
belly rising,
belly compressing,
conscious focus,
mind, body, breath
One.
Thought arises
observe, release.
Another follows
like a long train,
cars of remembrance
and creation
follow
like unravelling thread.
Breathing in,
breathing out,
observe and release,
conscious focus
One.

2017

THE BOX WITHOUT A LID

This mind and this body
Create the box.

Experience, notions,
Perceptions, and conceptions
Fill the box.

Time renders useless
What has been stored,
And a gradual discard begins.

As the burden
Of what has been held
Is released and given away,
The walls of the box
Collapse into emptiness
And true freedom awakens.

2020

CORONA VIRUS

The Corona Virus
Is the wind
Blowing all dead and useless living
From the grasp of humanity,
Rendering us bare and new
To begin again.

2020

EVAPORATION
The end of a relationship

The arrival brings a fullness of expectation,
Dreams, anticipation, excitement,
Newness and possibility.
The unknown creates an internal dialogue
Of clinging and discarding,
Of manifesting and rewriting the heart's desires.
The waters of daily living
Slowly wash away the debris
Of what is not true.
The heat of realization
Dries up the hopes and dreams
And leaves the relationship standing
On a dry bed of extinction.

2020

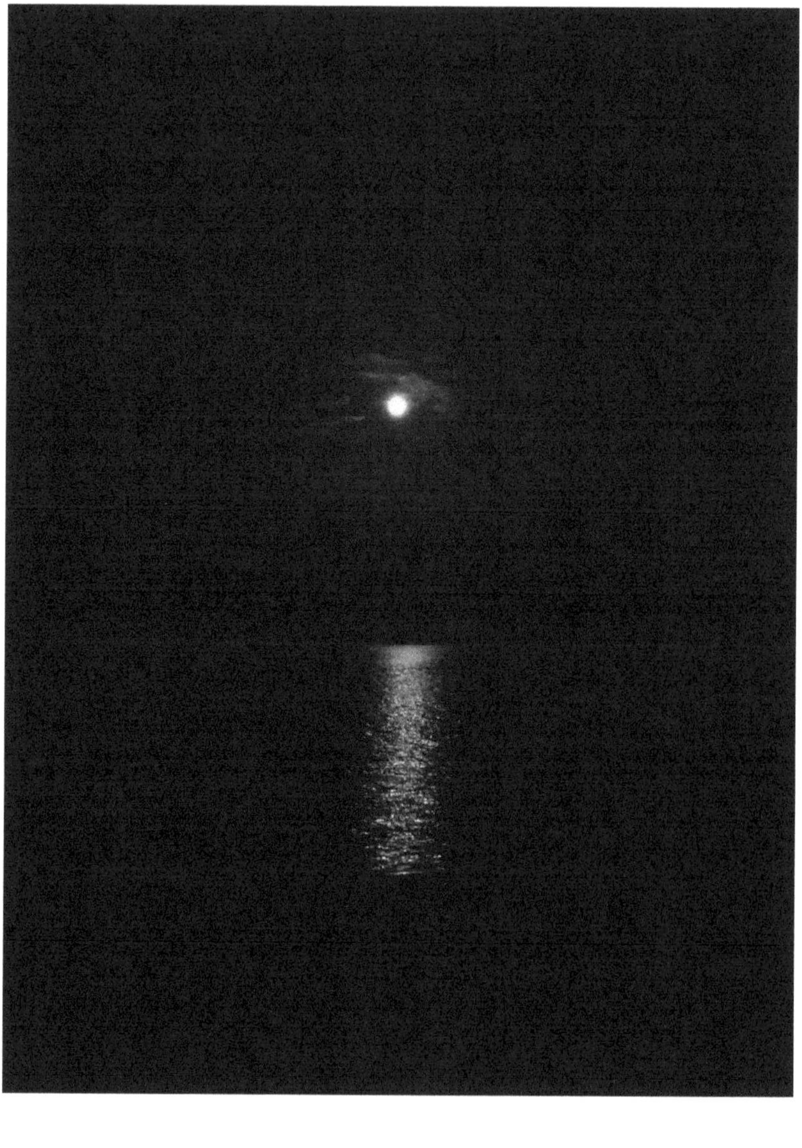

THE JAILER

Here I sit
In the prison of my thoughts,
My notions, conceptions,
Perceptions, and judgements,
Trapped under the weight
Of what I hold tightly to be true.

Exhausted and weary,
I surrender.

The release of my burden
Cracks open the emptiness
Of my thoughts,
My notions, conceptions,
Perceptions, and judgements.

The door swings open...
And I am free.

2020

A LOVE LETTER HOME

Dearest,
At a very young age
I followed the voices of the world.
Distracted, I ignored your guiding messages.
Lost, I looked everywhere but inside.
Now at the age of redemption,
I see you.
I feel you.
I hear you.
I embrace the gifts of genetics and ancestry.
I marvel at your strength and endurance.
I smile and kiss the weathered structure
That brought my babies to life
And kept me strong and healthy
Despite my choices.
Thank you for calling me home.
I love you!

2020

LOVING FOR DUMMIES

Step One:

Be the first in line
Love yourself
Forgive yourself
Do not judge or criticize yourself
Laugh at yourself
Nurture yourself
Feed yourself
Hold yourself
Talk to yourself
Appreciate yourself
Thank yourself
Accept yourself
Be grateful to yourself
Smile to yourself
Hug yourself
Dance with yourself
Amaze yourself

Step Two:

Turn around and give it all away.

2020

REFLECTION

Who is this woman in the mirror?
Oh, the shadows are lifting.
I see her so clear.
All my relations
Are present here.

2020

PERFECTION

"I am not beautiful," you might say,
"This is not right,"
or "I don't like that."
Your thoughts and perceptions
are creating a picture
you think is not perfect.
What is perfection?
Who or what decides this idea of perfection?
You do!
Open your eyes, and take a closer look.

When you are standing in nature,
enjoying all it has to offer,
you don't say
"That stone is the wrong shape"
or "That tree has an ugly branch."
No, you accept everything
just as it is,
and that is where your beauty begins,
with acceptance,
just as you are.

2020

THE PRESENT

*B*eautiful child, young and old, let me share with you what I have learned. We travel this physical journey on earth in a magnificent vehicle with three engines: the mind, the body, and the soul. Each is important to the others, and when running in harmony, brings great joy to ourselves and the world we live in.

The body allows us to see, hear, touch, taste, smell, and move. The mind creates the thoughts and stories as we experience, moment to moment, this world we are living in. The soul is truth and knowing, the present of life. The soul is the great editor of the stories we create and what is false and what is true.

The fuel that keeps our engines running is our breath. Breathing in, we energize and idle smoothly. Breathing out, we cleanse and release impurities. In the stillness of breathing in and out—focusing on the gentle hum and vibration of our breath—mind gradually releases thoughts, body gradually releases tensions, and the soul speaks ever so softly in knowing.

It takes practice and patience, but it is a present well worth unwrapping. It has always been here, waiting for us to open. There is no time like the present. The present is now.

2020

CONCERTINA

I am a concertina
Played by the hands of God,
Stretching out, drawing in
The energies of heaven and earth
To the bellows of my heart.
Squeezing out,
Sharing the music of my soul
With the chorus of all,
One in our songs
Of love and sorrow,
Joy and sadness,
Anger and frustration,
Peace and freedom.
I am a concertina
Played by the hands of God,
And these are my songs.

2020

Such a pursuit
to discover and define myself
only to realize
there is no
"me"

2020

And time washes the pain and suffering
From the tapestry of my life,
Leaving the unique texture of experience
Aglow in the beautiful colours of understanding.

$\mathscr{K}$imella Hilliard lives in the village of Saanichton on beautiful Vancouver Island in British Columbia. She is enjoying the complete freedom of retirement and exploring her creative passions, which she neglected to give her full attention to before now.

CPSIA information can be obtained
at www.ICGtesting.com
Printed in the USA
BVHW052022050921
615941BV00003B/10

9 781039 115064